INJUSTICE

GODS AMONG US: YEAR TWO

VOLUME 1

INJU

GODS AMO

Tom Taylor
Writer

**Bruno Redondo Julien Hugonnard-Bert
Mike S. Miller Saleem Crawford**
Artists

**David Lopez & Santi Casas of Ikari Studio
Rex Lokus**
Colorists

Wes Abbott
Letterer

**Jheremy Raapack with
David Lopez & Santi Casas of Ikari Studio**
Cover Artists

STICE

U S : YEAR TWO

VOLUME 1

Jim Chadwick Editor – Original Series
Aniz Ansari Assistant Editor – Original Series
Rachel Pinnelas Editor
Robbin Brosterman Design Director – Books
Louis Prandi Publication Design

Hank Kanalz Senior VP – Vertigo & Integrated Publishing

Diane Nelson President
Dan DiDio and Jim Lee Co-Publishers
Geoff Johns Chief Creative Officer
Amit Desai Senior VP – Marketing & Franchise Management
Amy Genkins Senior VP – Business & Legal Affairs
Nairi Gardiner Senior VP – Finance
Jeff Boison VP – Publishing Planning
Mark Chiarello VP – Art Direction & Design
John Cunningham VP – Marketing
Terri Cunningham VP – Editorial Administration
Larry Ganem VP – Talent Relations & Services
Alison Gill Senior VP – Manufacturing & Operations
Jay Kogan VP – Business & Legal Affairs, Publishing
Jack Mahan VP – Business Affairs, Talent
Nick Napolitano VP – Manufacturing Administration
Sue Pohja VP – Book Sales
Fred Ruiz VP – Manufacturing Operations
Courtney Simmons Senior VP – Publicity
Bob Wayne Senior VP – Sales

INJUSTICE: GODS AMONG US: YEAR TWO VOLUME 1

Published by DC Comics. Copyright © 2014 DC Comics. All Rights
Reserved.

Originally published in single magazine form in INJUSTICE YEAR TWO
1-6 Copyright © 2014 DC Comics. All Rights Reserved. All characters,
their distinctive likenesses and related elements featured in this
publication are trademarks of DC Comics. The stories, characters and
incidents featured in this publication are entirely fictional. DC Comics
does not read or accept unsolicited ideas, stories or artwork.

DC Comics, 1700 Broadway, New York, NY 10019
A Warner Bros. Entertainment Company.
Printed by RR Donnelley, Salem, VA, USA. 8/22/14.
First Printing.

ISBN: 978-1-4012-5071-3

Library of Congress Cataloging-in-Publication Data

Taylor, Tom, 1978- author.
  Injustice : Gods Among Us Year 2 Volume 1 / Tom Taylor, Mike S. Miller
    pages cm
ISBN 978-1-4012-5071-3 (hardback)
  1. Graphic novels. I. Miller, Mike S., illustrator. II. Derenick, Tom,
illustrator. III. Title. IV. Title: Gods Among Us Year 2 Volume 1.
  PN6727.T293I58 2014
  741.5'973—dc23
                                2014011937

THE STORY SO FAR

When the Joker ditches Gotham and heads for Metropolis, Superman and Lois Lane are the victims of his most sinister plot to date. The aftermath unleashes an atomic explosion that destroys the City of Tomorrow, and with it Lois Lane and their unborn child. Mad with grief, the Man of Steel does the unthinkable and murders the Joker in cold blood as Batman looks on in horror. When Superman is willing to commit atrocities, who can possibly stand against him?

Superman begins a campaign to end violence the world over, involving himself in civil wars and international conflict. Batman warns that this level of intervention is a slippery slope towards a police state, but the Justice League sides with Clark. After a tense conflict with Aquaman over who holds authority over the oceans, some members question their actions and, like Batman, feel that they're overstepping their bounds.

As their peacekeeping efforts increase, the Justice League ends up at war with their own government, who attempt to use Jonathan and Martha Kent as leverage against the Man of Steel. When the League starts taking the inmates at Arkham to somewhere more secure, a terrible accident takes the life of Nightwing. A broken Bruce Wayne tries to cope with the death with the help of Catwoman, and the two work toward a solution to the increasingly oppressive activities of Superman.

The Justice League finds one unlikely survivor of the Metropolis massacre, Lex Luthor, safe within his fallout shelter, and he joins their efforts to save the planet. But Superman is again forced to escalate what he is willing to do to protect Earth when an invasion from Apokolips led by Kalibak overtakes Earth. Vaporizing the oncoming forces from space leads to widespread celebration of Superman, despite the carnage.

But Batman is still plotting against his old friend. When it's revealed that Batman has been in league with Martian Manhunter to spy on the Justice League, Superman responds by outing Bruce Wayne as Batman. Bruce then retaliates by knocking out power to the Watchtower, sending it hurtling to Earth from orbit. The resulting conflict leads to the death of Martian Manhunter at the hands of Superman.

Batman and his resistance team try for one last-ditch effort to get their hands on a Kryptonite-powered pill that grants super powers to give them a weapon in the fight against Superman. They succeed, but at the cost of Green Arrow and Captain Atom, and Bruce is badly injured in his fight with Clark. Superman and the remaining Justice League members then swear before the U.N. to defend Earth not only from themselves, but also from Batman and his allies.

--AND THE FINEST THIRD WHEEL A MAN AND HIS GIRL COULD HAVE."

NOW.

OLIVER QUEEN

LOVING HUSBAND
FRIEND
HERO

"YOU ARE IN THE TOWER OF DOCTOR FATE."

I CAN'T STAY HERE. I HAVE TO--

SHHH.

TSER, ECURB ENYAW.

ESOLC RUOY SEYE DNA PEELS.

WHAT...?

WHAT HAPPENED?

I GOT IT BACK UNDER CONTROL.

HOW?

SKILL. TALENT.

I SAW THE READOUT. THE PLANE WAS DEAD IN THE SKY.

SHOW ME YOUR HAND.

WHAT?

SHOW ME.

WOULD YOU PREFER TO HAVE MILLIONS OF DOLLARS OF JET IN FLAMING PIECES ACROSS YOUR RUNWAY? WITH SOME CHUNKS OF FORMERLY-HANDSOME PILOT MIXED IN?

HAL. CONGRESS IS ABOUT TO SHUT DOWN THE U.S. GOVERNMENT.

AND YOU WANT ME TO DO WHAT, EXACTLY?

I WANT YOU TO CONVINCE THEM NOT TO.

YOU ARE THE GREEN LANTERN OF SECTOR 2814. YOU HAVE BEEN CHARGED WITH SAFEGUARDING EARTH AND ITS PEOPLE. THIS IS NOT INTERFERENCE. THIS IS PROTECTION.

THAT LEVEL OF INTERFERENCE--

WELL, IT'S HARD TO ARGUE WITH THAT.

ANY CHANGE IN DIANA?

KRYPTON. THEN.

THE HALL OF JUSTICE.
EARTH.

WHAT CAN I DO FOR YOU, GANTHET?

YOU HAVE HELPED US MANY TIMES IN THE PAST. THERE HAVE BEEN TIMES WHEN YOUR INTERVENTION WAS THE DIFFERENCE BETWEEN VICTORY AND DEFEAT, AND SO I COME TO YOU TODAY AS A FRIEND--AS AN AMBASSADOR OF OA.

I AM HERE TO ADVISE. NOT TO INTERFERE.

AND WHAT IS YOUR ADVICE?

STOP WHAT YOU ARE DOING.

WHAT I'M DOING IS PROTECTING THESE PEOPLE.

NO, SUPERMAN. WHAT YOU ARE DOING IS SEEKING TO CONTROL THEM.

I AM ONE OF THEM.

NO. YOU ARE NOT. YOU HAVE BEEN RAISED AMONG THEM BUT YOU ARE NOT OF EARTH.

YOU'RE RIGHT. I AM NOT OF THIS PLANET. MY PLANET WAS DESTROYED AND MY PEOPLE PERISHED DUE TO IGNORANT AND ARROGANT LEADERS NOT ACTING WHEN NEEDED.

I WILL NOT ALLOW THAT TO HAPPEN AGAIN.

I HAVE WATCHED MANY CIVILIZATIONS RISE AND FALL. WE GUARDIANS ARE GIFTED WITH ENORMOUS POWER. SOMETIMES, NOT USING THAT POWER IS THE MOST DIFFICULT DECISION OF ALL.

THE PEOPLE OF EARTH *MUST* BE ALLOWED TO FOLLOW THEIR OWN PATH, *WITHOUT* OUTSIDE INTERFERENCE OR CONTROL.

ASK HIM. ASK HIM *THE* QUESTION.

YOU SAID YOU HAVE WATCHED CIVILIZATIONS RISE AND FALL--

I AM SORRY TO SEE YOU LIKE THIS, SUPERMAN. IT IS CLEAR THAT YOU ARE PAST THE POINT OF REASON.

WE WILL RETURN TO OA. COME, HAL JORDAN.

I...

YOU REALIZE NOW WHAT I REALIZED LONG AGO. THEY ARE GUARDIANS IN NAME ONLY.

I AM SORRY FOR KRYPTON AND ITS PEOPLE, SUPERMAN.

YOU SEE NOW?

DO NOT THINK FOR A SECOND THAT I TRUST YOU, SINESTRO.

WE ARE NOT SO DIFFERENT, SUPERMAN. THEY WILL COME FOR YOU AS THEY CAME FOR ME.

I DON'T EXPECT YOU TO *TRUST* ME, BUT YOU WILL *NEED* ME WHEN THEY COME.

THE OCEAN PLANET
OF LANDWEND.

KILOWOG.

YEAH?

RETURN TO OA.

XUNDAR.

TOMAR RE. RETURN TO OA.

THE SOULE NEBULA.

ARISIA RRAB. RETURN TO OA.

RYUT. SPACE SECTOR 0666.

JOHN STEWART.

"...AND WE'VE CHOSEN GOTHAM AS THE FIRST CITY ON EARTH TO RECEIVE THIS UNIQUE PROTECTION."

A CONSTANTLY PATROLLING SECURITY FORCE OF ENHANCED PEOPLE, MISTER MAYOR.

IT'S NOT THAT GOTHAM DOESN'T APPRECIATE THE HELP--

"--I'M JUST NOT SURE COMMISSIONER GORDON AND HIS POLICE FORCE WILL SEE IT THE SAME WAY."

I DON'T CARE HOW HE SEES IT. GOTHAM IS A BLIGHT ON THIS COUNTRY. JIM GORDON HAS BEEN THE COMMISSIONER OF POLICE TO A CITY WITH THE WORST CRIME RATE IN THE COUNTRY.

ELL ME
U HAVE
PLAN."

IT'S YOUR DAD.

LET ME IN.

I THOUGHT THIS WAS A SECURE LOCATION. HOW DID HE FIND YOU?

I KNOW YOU'RE HERE, BARBARA.

CAM 09

I KNOW EVERYTHING.

I'M TELLING YOU THIS IS PRETTY MUCH THE WORST IDEA EVER.

THE HALL OF JUSTICE.

I REALIZE THAT THIS MAY SEEM UNWISE.

NO. IN THE TIME IT TOOK YOU TO SAY THAT SENTENCE, I EVALUATED THIS OVER THREE HUNDRED TIMES. AND I CAN TELL YOU THAT WE'RE WAY PAST 'UNWISE' AND ALL THE WAY INTO 'STUPID.'

I HAVE TO AGREE.

HE CAME HERE TO WARN US, LEX. WE MAY NEED HIM.

HE'S DANGEROUS.

THEY'RE RIGHT, SUPERMAN--

THEN.

"THEY TOLD ME I WAS THE GREATEST GREEN LANTERN.

"AND I BELIEVED IT. I BELIEVED I SHOULD DO MY BEST FOR THE GUARDIANS. I DID THEIR BIDDING, NO MATTER WHAT IT COST ME.

HNGG!

"NEVER QUESTIONING THE GUARDIANS' MOTIVES. DOING ALL I COULD FOR THEIR ATTENTION, FOR THEIR SCRAPS OF RECOGNITION.

"I THOUGHT I WAS THEIR HERO. THEY MADE ME BELIEVE THIS. BUT THEY ARE COLD AND UNFEELING. THEY DIDN'T SEE ME AS A HERO. I WAS A TOOL, A WEAPON TO BE WIELDED IN THEIR FIGHT FOR CONTROL OF THE UNIVERSE.

"THEY GAVE ME A SECTOR OF SPACE TO PATROL. KORUGAR, MY PLANET, WAS PART OF THIS.

"AND, HAVING BEEN HANDED THIS POWER, I COULD SEE ALL THAT WAS WRONG ON MY WORLD, AND I COULD SEE HOW TO IMPROVE IT.

"I BEGAN TO CHANGE MY WORLD FOR THE BETTER. I STOPPED PROTECTING THE STATUS QUO AND BEGAN CUTTING OUT THE ROT.

"AND NOWHERE WAS MORE ROTTEN THAN OUR CAPITAL."

AAAAGHH!!

"I WAS ABLE TO BRING DOWN OUR RULING GOVERNMENT, THE MEN AND WOMEN WHO HAD FAILED KORUGAR FOR SO LONG."

LOOK DOWN AT YOUR FEET. YOU DON'T DESERVE TO LOOK INTO THE FACES OF THE PEOPLE!

"AND THE PEOPLE LOVED ME FOR IT."

"I WAS MAKING A BETTER WORLD FOR MY FAMILY. FOR ARIN. FOR OUR DAUGHTER."

THIS IS OUR NEW HOME NOW, SORANIK.

THE PEOPLE WHO RULED HERE ARE GONE. DADDY MADE THEM PAY.

"THEY WERE EVERYTHING TO ME."

WHAT HAPPENED?

SOME OF THE ROT REMAINED. MY WIFE MUST HAVE SEEN THEM COMING BECAUSE SHE SENT OUR DAUGHTER INTO HIDING WHILE I WAS OFF-WORLD.

THE GUARDIANS HAD SENT ME FAR AWAY FROM MY FAMILY. I WAS DEALING WITH THE PROBLEMS OF ANOTHER WORLD. I WAS SAVING OTHER LIVES--

"DESPITE MY GRIEF, I CONTINUED TO HELP KORUGAR. I GAVE MYSELF TO THE PEOPLE.

"AND THEN THEY CAME.

"THOSE I'D TRAINED. MEN AND WOMEN WHO STOOD SHOULDER TO SHOULDER WITH ME FOR YEARS."

YOU WANNA EXPLAIN WHAT'S HAPPENING HERE, POOZER? 'CAUSE IT DOESN'T LOOK GOOD.

"I TRIED, SUPERMAN. I SERVED THE PEOPLE. I BROUGHT PEACE. I TRIUMPHED THROUGH TRAGEDY AND SAVED KORUGAR.

"AFTER EVERYTHIN[G] [I] DID, THE GUARDIA[NS] TURNED MY CLOS[EST] FRIENDS AGAINST

"HE WAS THE ONE TO FINALLY STRIP ME OF MY POWERS."

WHAT HAVE YO[U] TURNE[D] INTO?

"HIS WAS THE ULTIMATE BETRAYAL."

THIS WON'T STOP ME! I WILL TEAR YOUR CORPS APART!!

BUT I DON'T BLAME HAL JORDAN. I KNOW WHAT THE GUARDIANS DID. THEY POISONED HIS MIND. HE WAS THEIR TOOL.

IT IS ALMOST IMPOSSIBLE TO RESIST THEM.

YOU WILL DISCOVER THIS SOON. THEY'RE COMING FOR YOU.

OH, COME ON. CAN WE PLEASE NOT EVEN PRETEND TO BELIEVE THIS 'POOR MISUNDERSTOOD SINESTRO' SOB STORY? THIS IS THE POSTER BOY FOR AN ENTIRE CORPS OF EVIL, WHO SPEND ALL THEIR TIME DOING EVIL.

OA, HOME OF THE GUARDIANS OF THE UNIVERSE AND THEIR GREEN LANTERN CORPS.

I UNDERSTAND THE COUNCIL'S FEARS. AN UNCONTROLLED AND TYRANNICAL SUPERMAN WOULD REPRESENT A GREAT DANGER.

BUT YOU'RE MISJUDGING HIS ACTIONS. HE'S NOT ACTING FOR HIMSELF. HE IS STILL, AS HE ALWAYS HAS BEEN, FIGHTING FOR PEACE.

THE MAN I CONFRONTED ON EARTH WAS NOT A MAN ACTING PEACEFULLY.

THE MAN YOU CONFRONTED ON EARTH WAS ACTING JUST FINE UNTIL HE DISCOVERED THAT YOU WERE COMPLICIT IN THE DESTRUCTION OF HIS HOME PLANET.

IF YOU WANT TO JUDGE HIM, MAYBE YOU AND THE REST OF THE GUARDIANS SHOULD LOOK AT YOUR OWN ACTIONS HERE.

IT'S OVER.

STOP FIGHTING, HAL!

JOHN. SUPERMAN IS SAVING LIVES. HE IS SAVING OUR WORLD! THE GUARDIANS CANNOT BE ALLOWED TO--

THD

HNF!

YOU THINK YOU'RE STRONG, KILOWOG? HARD WORK PUMMELLING A GUY WITH HIS HANDS HELD BEHIND HIS BACK?

LET HIM GO!

NO.

IS TRYING TO BAIT YOU, OWOG. DO NOT LET YOUR RIDE OVERCOME YOUR REASON. END THIS.

THAT'S IT, TOUGH GUY. LISTEN TO YOUR PUPPET MASTERS. HIT THE DEFENSELESS. BE A HERO.

END THIS. NOW.

WHAT ARE *YOU* DOING HERE?

I'VE BEEN SENT TO RELIEVE YOU.

I WASN'T NOTIFIED OF THIS.

THE GUARDIANS LET YOU IN ON ALL OF THEIR PLANS NOW, SALAAK?

HOW'S THE PRISONER?

MOSTLY ARGUMENTATIVE. BUT SEE FOR YOURS--

THNK

...WHICH YOU'LL FIND BY TURNING TO PAGE THIRTY-SEVEN.

I'M SORRY TO INTERRUPT--

Miss Mooney

FAWCETT CITY HIGH SCHOOL

--BUT I NEED TO TALK TO BILLY.

UH...

BILLY BATSON...?

THANK YOU, MISS MOONEY.

HE'LL BE BACK AT SCHOOL TOMORROW.

UM... SUPERMAN? BEFORE YOU GO, DO YOU HAVE ANY WORDS FOR THE STUDENTS?

OF COURSE.

BE GOOD.

THE HALL OF JUSTICE.

"SOMEONE HAS TO STOP HIM, GUY."

OKAY. LET'S WRAP THIS UP.

WHAT ABOUT THESE TWO?

BRING THEM. WE'LL LET THE GUARDIANS DECIDE WHAT TO DO WITH THEM.

'P. CAN YOU KEEP ERMAN'S BRAIN OUT ACTION UNTIL WE GET TO OA?

SHLIK

SURE. L EVEN NOT TO MANENTLY MAGE HIM.

CH'P?

CH'P!

YOU...

OH, DON'T LOOK AT ME LIKE THAT, "POOZER." I DID YOU A FAVOR. YOU ALWAYS LOOKED RIDICULOUS FIGHTING BESIDE A SQUIRREL.

"--WHAT THE HELL IS HAPPENING DOWN THERE?"

SINESTRO!

BULLOCK?

HOW ARE YOU FEELING, DETECTIVE?

HOW DO YOU THINK I'M FEELING?

POLICE BEATEN IN THE STREET AND NO ONE WE CAN LOCK UP FOR IT?

I'M PRETTY MUCH AS PISSED AS I'VE EVER BEEN.

GOOD. GET UP.

COMMISSIONER?

"T'S BOILING OVER OUT THERE."

SUPERSOLDIERS OUT OF GOTHAM

SUPERSOLDIERS OUT OF GOTHAM

SUPER SOLDIERS OUT OF GOTHAM

SUPERSOLDIERS GO HOME!!!

GOTHAM CITY NOT GOTHAM PRISON

ALL PUBLIC GATHERINGS HAVE BEEN BANNED.

LEAVE HERE AT ONCE AND GO BACK TO YOUR HOMES!

NO. *YOU* LEAVE. GOTHAM IS *OUR* HOME.

GOTHAM BAN

"SUPERMAN DOESN'T UNDERSTAND.

"GOTHAM WON'T JUST SIT STILL WHILE SUPER-POWERED THUGS TAKE OVER THE CITY."

YOU STUPID--

CRACK

"HE THINKS MARCHING SOLDIERS IN, DECLARING CURFEWS AND BEATING PEOPLE UP WILL RESULT IN ORDER."

PUT HER DOWN, YOU #@&$!

"BUT GOTHAM CITIZENS HAVE NEVER BEEN KNOWN FOR THEIR COMPLIANCE."

SOUTH DAKOTA.